The Jacqueline Wilson Journal

Illustrated
by Nick
Sharratt

DOUBLEDAY

Here is
a photo
of me

This Jacqueline Wilson
Journal belongs to:

Name ....

....

Address ....

....

....

....

....

Phone number ....

....

Birthdate ....

....

....

E-mail address ....

....

Jacqueline's Favourites

Favourite food
Fruit — but cakes and chips when I'm feeling wicked

Favourite colour
Black and silver. I always wear black clothes — and I've got silver glasses and lots of silver jewellery

Favourite sport
Swimming — I do 50 lengths of my local pool every morning

Favourite time of day
Midnight — when I'm sitting up reading in bed

Favourite pen
A big ornate black and silver pen (a present from my daughter Emma)

Favourite place to go for a walk
Home Park — especially in the autumn when there are toadstools the size of dinner plates

Favourite animal
Lemur

Favourite book
Lavender's Blue,
a nursery rhyme book illustrated by Harold Jones

Favourite smell
Roses

Favourite thing to wear
Black velvet

Favourite music
Queen, Anonymous 4, Dory Previn, Mary Chapin Carpenter, Renee Fleming, Michael Nyman

Favourite place to go on holiday
Boston in America

Favourite character in Jacqueline Wilson's books!
Dolphin in *The Illustrated Mum,*
though I'm very fond of Biscuits
in *Cliffhanger, Buried Alive* and *Best Friends*

Nick's Favourites

Favourite food
Home-made trifle

Favourite colour
Bright yellow

Favourite sport
Skiing

Favourite time of day
Ten to four – home time when I was at school

Favourite pen
A pen that I've had since I was a boy
and that I use to write all my letters

Favourite place to go for a walk
Along the seafront in Brighton

Favourite animal
Elephant

Favourite book
The Giant Jam Sandwich by John Vernon Lord and Janet Burroway

Favourite smell
Cut grass

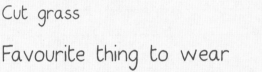

Favourite thing to wear
A battered old pair of loafers.
I can't draw properly unless I'm wearing them!

Favourite music
Music from James Bond films. And a song called 'The Day Before You Came' by Abba

Favourite place to go on holiday
Swaledale in North Yorkshire

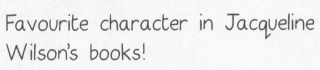

Favourite character in Jacqueline Wilson's books!
Charlie in *The Lottie Project* and Tanya in *Bad Girls*

My Favourites

Favourite food ....
....

Favourite colour ....
....

Favourite sport ....
....
....

Favourite time of day ....
....
....

Favourite pen ....
....

Favourite place to go for a walk ....
....

Favourite animal ....
....

Favourite book ....
....

Favourite smell ....
....

Favourite thing to wear ....
....

Favourite music
....
....

Favourite place to go on holiday ....
....
....

Favourite character in Jacqueline Wilson's books
....

My Ideal Weekend

I would get up at .... o'clock

I would wear......................................
....
....

I would go to ....
....
....
....

I would meet up with ....
....
....
....

I would see ....

....

....

I would eat ....

....

....

I would visit ....

....

....

In the evening I would ....

....

....

....

I would go to bed at .... o' clock

I would dream about ....

....

....

....

My Favourite Hopes and Dreams

....

....

....

....

....

....

....

....

....

....

....

....

....

....

....

....

....

....

....

....

....

Make Your Wishes Come True

GRIZELDA MOONBEAM
White Witch

My Worst Worries and Problems

....
....
....
....
....

....
....
....
....

....
....
....

....
....
....
....
....
....

My Predictions for the Future

In five years' time I will be ....
....
....
....
....

In ten years' time I shall be ....
....
....
....
....

My first job will be. ....
....
....

My ideal job would be ....

....

....

....

....

I shall have .... children

I shall live in ....

....

....

....

....

I shall live with ....

....

....

....

I am going to ....

....

....

....

1 JANUARY

2 JANUARY

3 JANUARY

4 JANUARY

5 JANUARY

6 JANUARY

7 JANUARY

8 JANUARY

9 JANUARY

10 JANUARY

11 JANUARY

12 JANUARY

13 JANUARY

14 JANUARY

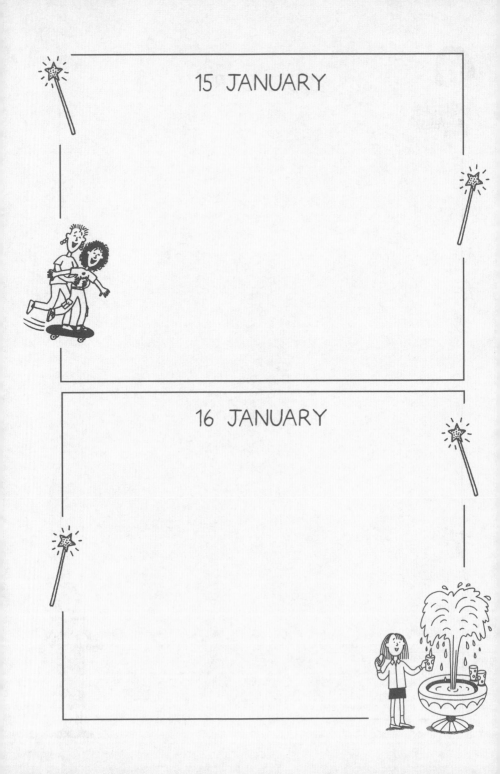

15 JANUARY

16 JANUARY

17 JANUARY

18 JANUARY

19 JANUARY

20 JANUARY

21 JANUARY

22 JANUARY

23 JANUARY

24 JANUARY

25 JANUARY

26 JANUARY

27 JANUARY

28 JANUARY

29 JANUARY

30 JANUARY

31 JANUARY

1 FEBRUARY

2 FEBRUARY

3 FEBRUARY

4 FEBRUARY

5 FEBRUARY

6 FEBRUARY

7 FEBRUARY

8 FEBRUARY

9 FEBRUARY

10 FEBRUARY

11 FEBRUARY

12 FEBRUARY

13 FEBRUARY

14 FEBRUARY

15 FEBRUARY

16 FEBRUARY

17 FEBRUARY

18 FEBRUARY

19 FEBRUARY

20 FEBRUARY

21 FEBRUARY

22 FEBRUARY

23 FEBRUARY

24 FEBRUARY

25 FEBRUARY

26 FEBRUARY

27 FEBRUARY

28 FEBRUARY

29 FEBRUARY
Leap year only

1 MARCH

2 MARCH

3 MARCH

4 MARCH

5 MARCH

6 MARCH

7 MARCH

8 MARCH

9 MARCH

10 MARCH

11 MARCH

12 MARCH

13 MARCH

14 MARCH

15 MARCH

16 MARCH

17 MARCH

18 MARCH

19 MARCH

20 MARCH

21 MARCH

22 MARCH

23 MARCH

24 MARCH

25 MARCH

26 MARCH

27 MARCH

28 MARCH

29 MARCH

30 MARCH

31 MARCH

1 APRIL

2 APRIL

3 APRIL

4 APRIL

5 APRIL

6 APRIL

7 APRIL

8 APRIL

9 APRIL

10 APRIL

11 APRIL

12 APRIL

13 APRIL

14 APRIL

15 APRIL

16 APRIL

17 APRIL

18 APRIL

19 APRIL

20 APRIL

21 APRIL

22 APRIL

23 APRIL

24 APRIL

25 APRIL

26 APRIL

27 APRIL

28 APRIL

29 APRIL

30 APRIL

1 MAY

2 MAY

3 MAY

4 MAY

5 MAY

6 MAY

7 MAY

8 MAY

9 MAY

10 MAY

11 MAY

12 MAY

13 MAY

14 MAY

15 MAY

16 MAY

17 MAY

18 MAY

19 MAY

20 MAY

21 MAY

22 MAY

23 MAY

24 MAY

25 MAY

26 MAY

27 MAY

28 MAY

29 MAY

30 MAY

31 MAY

1 JUNE

2 JUNE

3 JUNE

4 JUNE

5 JUNE

6 JUNE

7 JUNE

8 JUNE

9 JUNE

10 JUNE

11 JUNE

12 JUNE

13 JUNE

14 JUNE

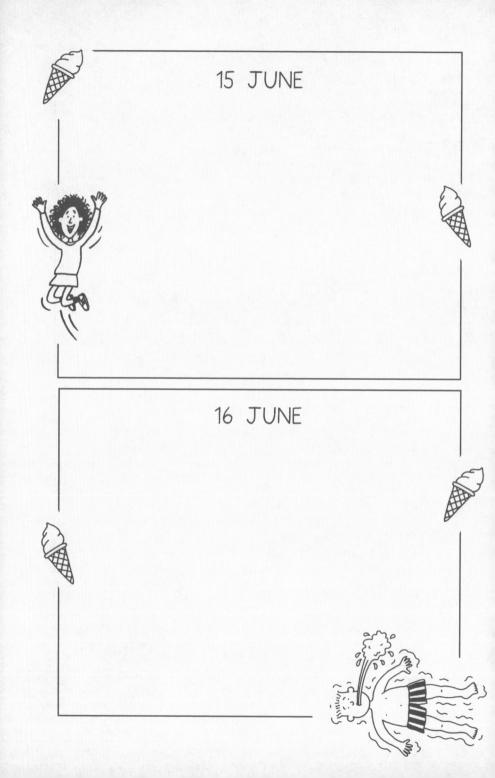

15 JUNE

16 JUNE

17 JUNE

18 JUNE

19 JUNE

20 JUNE

21 JUNE

22 JUNE

23 JUNE

24 JUNE

25 JUNE

26 JUNE

27 JUNE

28 JUNE

29 JUNE

30 JUNE

1 JULY

2 JULY

3 JULY

4 JULY

5 JULY

6 JULY

7 JULY

8 JULY

9 JULY

10 JULY

11 JULY

12 JULY

13 JULY

14 JULY

15 JULY

16 JULY

17 JULY

18 JULY

19 JULY

20 JULY

21 JULY

22 JULY

23 JULY

24 JULY

25 JULY

26 JULY

27 JULY

28 JULY

29 JULY

30 JULY

31 JULY

1 AUGUST

2 AUGUST

3 AUGUST

4 AUGUST

5 AUGUST

6 AUGUST

7 AUGUST

8 AUGUST

9 AUGUST

10 AUGUST

11 AUGUST

12 AUGUST

13 AUGUST

14 AUGUST

15 AUGUST

16 AUGUST

17 AUGUST

18 AUGUST

19 AUGUST

20 AUGUST

21 AUGUST

22 AUGUST

23 AUGUST

24 AUGUST

25 AUGUST

26 AUGUST

27 AUGUST

28 AUGUST

29 AUGUST

30 AUGUST

31 AUGUST

1 SEPTEMBER

2 SEPTEMBER

3 SEPTEMBER

4 SEPTEMBER

5 SEPTEMBER

6 SEPTEMBER

7 SEPTEMBER

8 SEPTEMBER

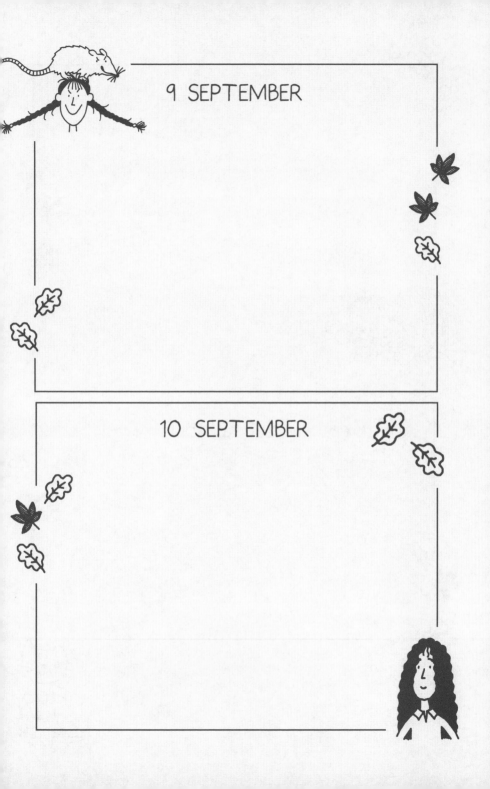

9 SEPTEMBER

10 SEPTEMBER

11 SEPTEMBER

12 SEPTEMBER

13 SEPTEMBER

14 SEPTEMBER

15 SEPTEMBER

16 SEPTEMBER

17 SEPTEMBER

18 SEPTEMBER

19 SEPTEMBER

20 SEPTEMBER

21 SEPTEMBER

22 SEPTEMBER

23 SEPTEMBER

24 SEPTEMBER

25 SEPTEMBER

26 SEPTEMBER

27 SEPTEMBER

28 SEPTEMBER

29 SEPTEMBER

30 SEPTEMBER

1 OCTOBER

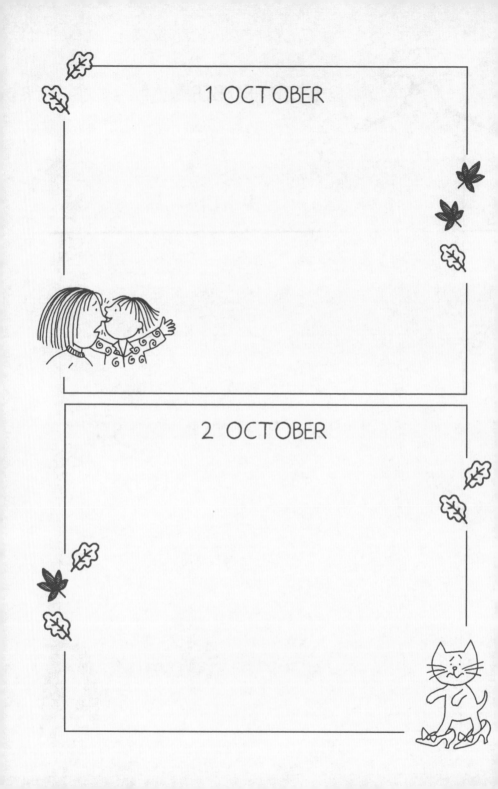

2 OCTOBER

3 OCTOBER

4 OCTOBER

5 OCTOBER

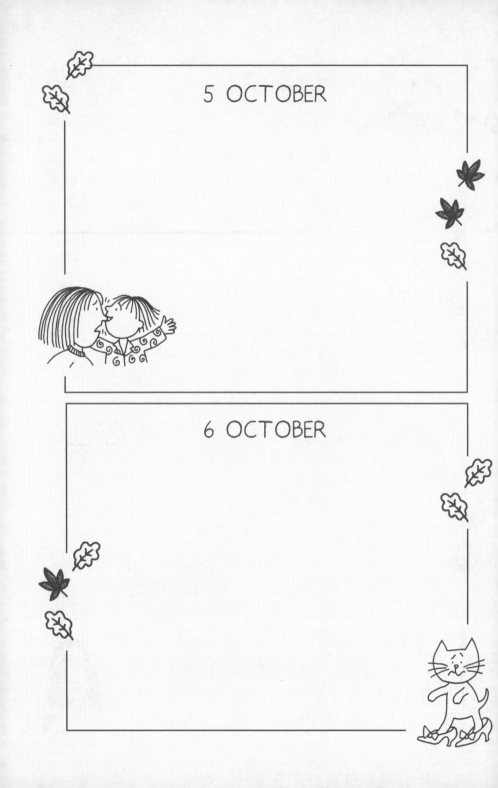

6 OCTOBER

7 OCTOBER

8 OCTOBER

9 OCTOBER

10 OCTOBER

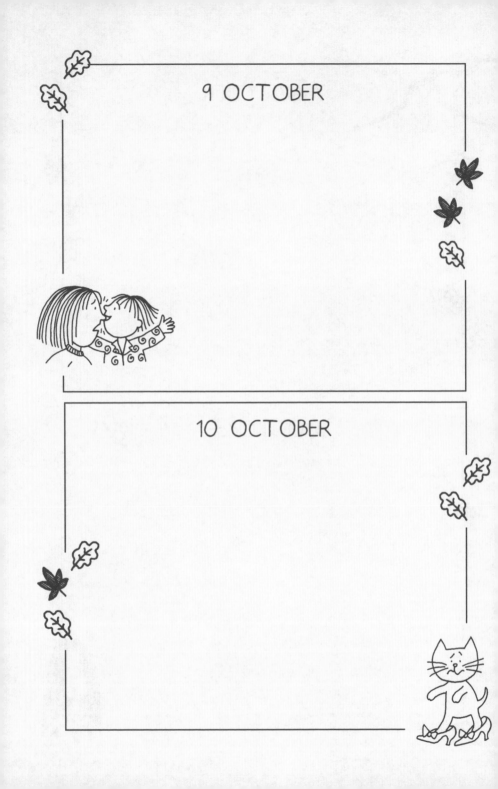

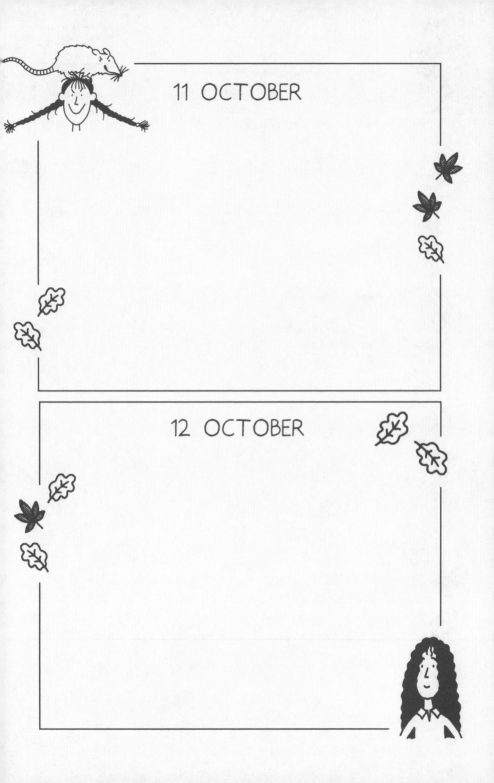

11 OCTOBER

12 OCTOBER

13 OCTOBER

14 OCTOBER

15 OCTOBER

16 OCTOBER

17 OCTOBER

18 OCTOBER

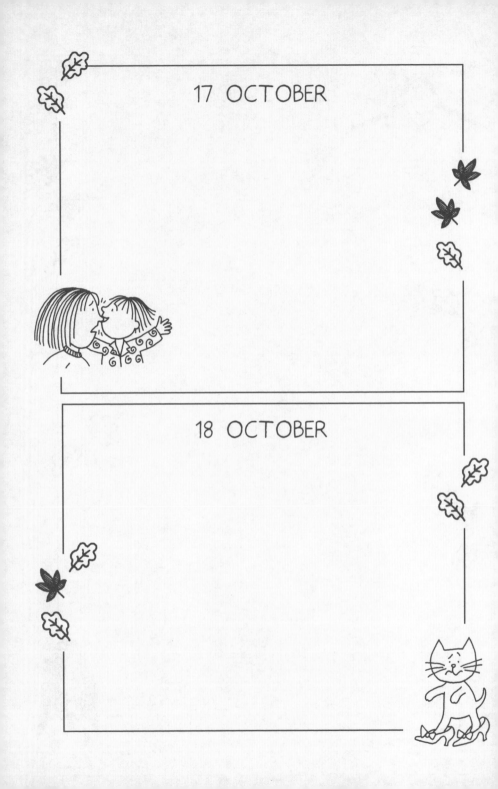

19 OCTOBER

20 OCTOBER

21 OCTOBER

22 OCTOBER

23 OCTOBER

24 OCTOBER

25 OCTOBER

26 OCTOBER

27 OCTOBER

28 OCTOBER

29 OCTOBER

30 OCTOBER

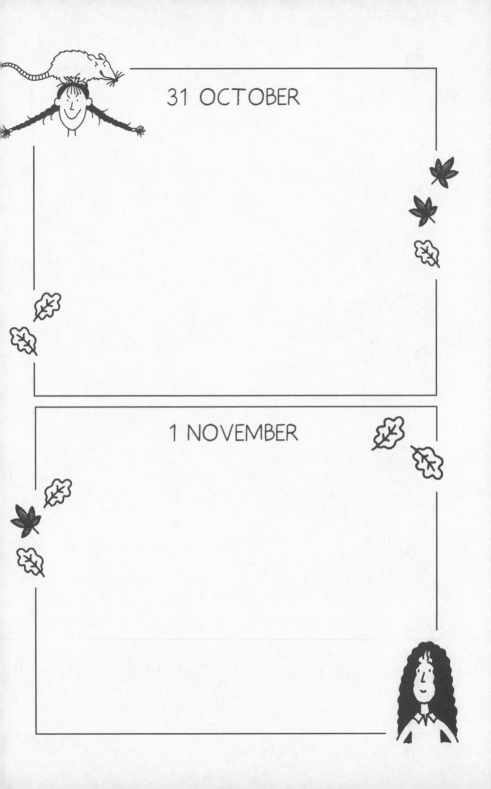

31 OCTOBER

1 NOVEMBER

2 NOVEMBER

3 NOVEMBER

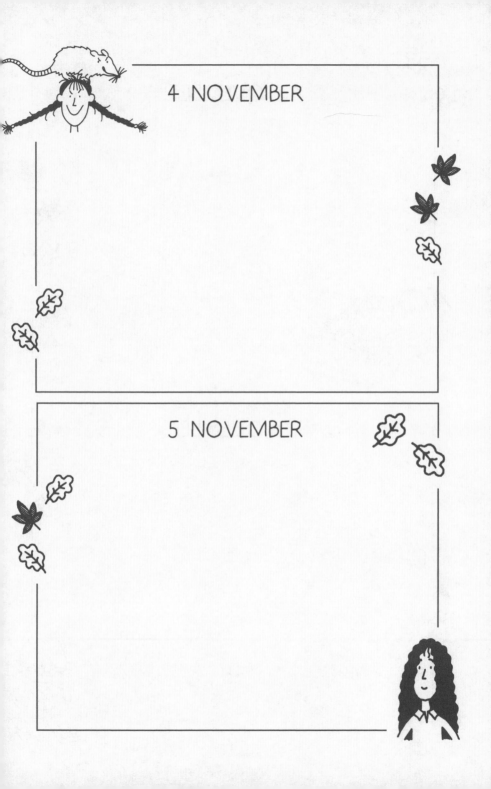

4 NOVEMBER

5 NOVEMBER

6 NOVEMBER

7 NOVEMBER

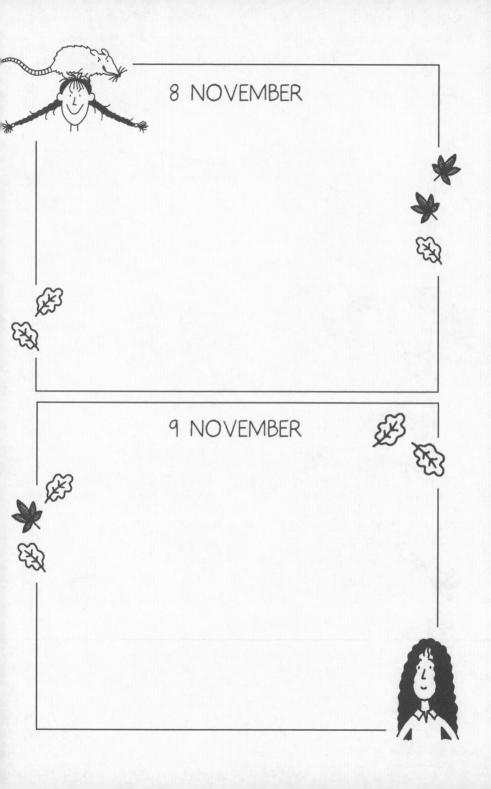

8 NOVEMBER

9 NOVEMBER

10 NOVEMBER

11 NOVEMBER

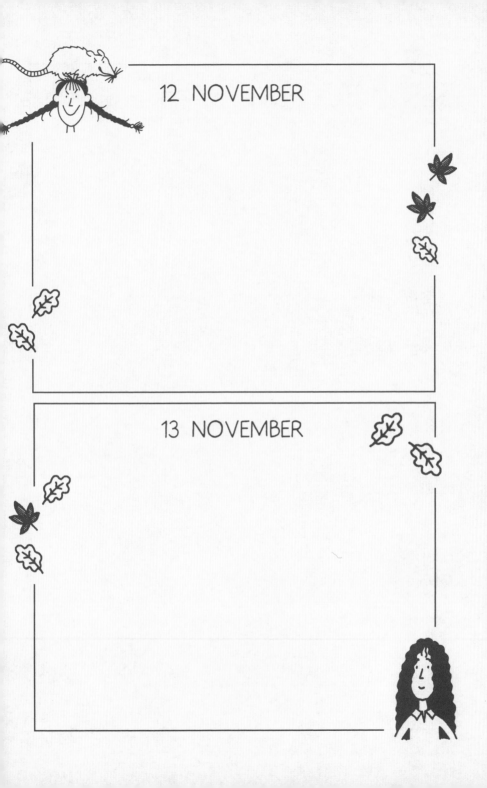

12 NOVEMBER

13 NOVEMBER

14 NOVEMBER

15 NOVEMBER

16 NOVEMBER

17 NOVEMBER

18 NOVEMBER

19 NOVEMBER

20 NOVEMBER

21 NOVEMBER

22 NOVEMBER

23 NOVEMBER

24 NOVEMBER

25 NOVEMBER

26 NOVEMBER

27 NOVEMBER

28 NOVEMBER

29 NOVEMBER

30 NOVEMBER

1 DECEMBER

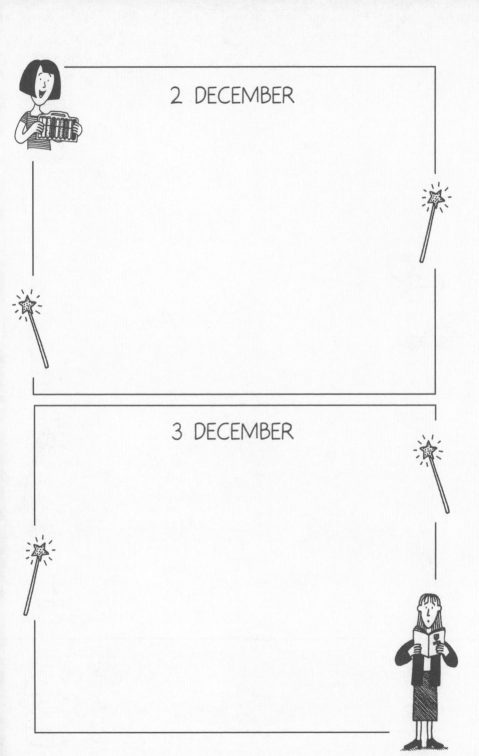

2 DECEMBER

3 DECEMBER

4 DECEMBER

5 DECEMBER

6 DECEMBER

7 DECEMBER

8 DECEMBER

9 DECEMBER

10 DECEMBER

11 DECEMBER

12 DECEMBER

13 DECEMBER

14 DECEMBER

15 DECEMBER

16 DECEMBER

17 DECEMBER

18 DECEMBER

19 DECEMBER

20 DECEMBER

21 DECEMBER

22 DECEMBER

23 DECEMBER

24 DECEMBER

25 DECEMBER

26 DECEMBER

27 DECEMBER

28 DECEMBER

29 DECEMBER

30 DECEMBER

31 DECEMBER

Jacky Daydream

by Jacqueline Wilson

Everybody knows Tracy Beaker, Jacqueline Wilson's best–loved character. But what do they know about the little girl who grew up to become Jacqueline Wilson?

How she played with paper dolls like April in *Dustbin Baby*.

How she dealt with an unpredictable father like Prue in *Love Lessons*.

How she chose new toys in Hamleys like Dolphin in The *Illustrated Mum*.

How she enjoyed Christmas like Em in *Clean Break*.

How she sat entrance exams like Ruby in *Double Act*.

But most of all how she loved reading and writing stories. Losing herself in a new world was the best possible way she could think of spending her time. From the very first story she wrote, *Meet the Maggots*, it was clear that this little girl had a very vivid imagination. But who would've guessed that she would grow up to be the mega-bestselling, award-winning Jacqueline Wilson!

Starring Tracy Beaker

by Jacqueline Wilson

Tracy Beaker is back . . . and she's just
desperate for a role in her school play.
They're performing *A Christmas Carol* and for
one worrying moment, the irrepressible Tracy
thinks she might not even get to play one of
the unnamed street urchins. But then she
is cast in the main role. Can she manage to act
grumpy and difficult enough to play Scrooge?
Well, she does have a bit of help on that front
from Justine Pain-In-The-Bum Littlewood . . .

As Tracy prepares for her big moment,
Cam is the one helping her learn her lines.
But all Tracy wants to know is if her film-star
mum will come to watch her in her starring role.

'Exciting and thrilling, funny and
full of suspense'   *First News*

Have you read all these
Jacqueline Wilson books?

Also available by Jacqueline Wilson

Published in Corgi Pups,
for beginner readers:

THE DINOSAUR'S PACKED LUNCH
THE MONSTER STORY-TELLER

Published in Young Corgi,
for newly confident readers:

LIZZIE ZIPMOUTH
SLEEPOVERS

Published in Doubleday/Corgi Yearling Books:

BAD GIRLS
THE BED & BREAKFAST STAR
BEST FRIENDS
BURIED ALIVE!
CANDYFLOSS
THE CAT MUMMY
CLEAN BREAK
CLIFFHANGER
THE DARE GAME
DOUBLE ACT
GLUBBSLYME
THE ILLUSTRATED MUM
JACKY DAYDREAM
THE LOTTIE PROJECT
MIDNIGHT
THE MUM-MINDER

SECRETS
STARRING TRACY BEAKER
THE STORY OF TRACY BEAKER
THE SUITCASE KID
VICKY ANGEL
THE WORRY WEBSITE

Collections:

THE JACQUELINE WILSON COLLECTION
includes THE STORY OF TRACY BEAKER and

THE BED AND BREAKFAST STAR
JACQUELINE WILSON'S DOUBLE-DECKER
includes BAD GIRLS and DOUBLE ACT

JACQUELINE WILSON'S SUPERSTARS
includes THE SUITCASE KID and
THE LOTTIE PROJECT

THE JACQUELINE WILSON BISCUIT BARREL
includes BURIED ALIVE and CLIFFHANGER

Available from Doubleday/Corgi Books,
for older readers:

THE DIAMOND GIRLS
DUSTBIN BABY
GIRLS IN LOVE
GIRLS OUT LATE
GIRLS UNDER PRESSURE
GIRLS IN TEARS
LOLA ROSE
LOVE LESSONS

Join the FREE online

Jacqueline Wilson

☆ FAN CLUB ☆

Read Jacqueline's monthly diary, look up

tour info, receive fan club e-newsletters.

All this and more, including members'

jokes and loads of exclusive top offers

Visit www.jacquelinewilson.co.uk

for more info!

THE JACQUELINE WILSON JOURNAL
A DOUBLEDAY BOOK 978 0 385 61327 9

Published in Great Britain by Doubleday,
an imprint of Random House Children's Books

Originally published in a different format in 2001
This edition published 2007

1 3 5 7 9 10 8 6 4 2

The Random House Group Limited makes every effort to ensure that the papers
used in its books are made from trees that have been legally sourced from
well-managed and credibly certified forests. Our paper procurement policy can
be found at: www.randomhouse.co.uk/paper.htm

RANDOM HOUSE CHILDREN'S BOOKS
61-63 Uxbridge Road, London W5 5SA

www.kidsatrandomhouse.co.uk

Addresses for companies within The Random House Group Limited
can be found at: www.randomhouse.co.uk/offices.htm

THE RANDOM HOUSE GROUP Limited Reg. No. 954009

A CIP catalogue record for this book is available from the British Library.

Printed and bound in Singapore